WHY CHRISTMAS TREES AREN'T PERFECT

WHY CHRISTMAS TREES AREN'T PERFECT

RICHARD H. SCHNEIDER

ILLUSTRATED BY

ELIZABETH J. MILES

Abingdon Press

Nashville

Library of Congress Cataloging-in-Publication Data

SCHNEIDER, DICK, 1922–
    Why Christmas trees aren't perfect / Dick Schneider. p. cm.
    Summary: Even though its kind sacrifices for the animals of the forest have marred the perfection of its shape, Small Pine is selected to be the Christmas tree in the Queen's castle, demonstrating that living for the sake of others makes us most beautiful in the eyes of God.
    ISBN 0-687-45363-1 (alk. paper)
    [1. Trees—Fiction. 2. Christmas trees—Fiction. 3. Kindness—Fiction. 4. Christian life—Fiction.] I. Title.
PZ7.S3624Wh   1987   [Fic]—dc19   87-20571

Printed in Hong Kong

00 01 02 03 04 — 20 19 18 17 16 15

hey say that if you creep into an evergreen forest late at night you can hear the trees talking. If you listen very carefully to the whisper of the wind, you can hear the older pines telling the younger ones why they will never be perfect. They will always have a bent branch here, a gap there. . . .

But long, long ago all ever-green trees *were* perfect. Each one took special pride in branches that sloped smoothly down from pointed top to evenly shaped skirt.

This was especially true in a small king-dom far beyond the Carpathian Mountains in Europe. Here the evergreen trees were the most beautiful of all. For here the sun shone just right, not too hot, not too dim. Here the rain fell just enough to keep the ground moist and soft so no tree went thirsty. And here the snow fell gently day after day to keep every branch fresh and green.

Each year as Christmas approached, the Queen's woodsmen would search the royal evergreen forest for the most perfect, most beautiful tree. The one fortunate enough to be chosen would be cut on the first Saturday of Advent. It would then be carefully carried to the castle and set up in the center of the great hall. There it reigned in honor for all the Christmas celebrations.

Out in the hushed forest every evergreen hoped for this honor. Each tree tried to grow its branches and needles to perfection. All of them strained to have the best form and appearance.

One tree, Small Pine, grew near the edge of the forest and promised to be the most beautiful of all. As a seedling it had listened carefully to the older trees who knew what was best for young saplings. And it had tried so very hard to grow just right. As a result, everything about Small Pine, from its deep sea-green color to the curling tip of its evenly spaced branches, was perfect.

It had, in fact, already overheard jealous whispers from the other trees. But it paid them no mind. Small Pine knew that if one did one's very best, what anyone else said didn't matter.

One cold night, when a bright full moon glittered on the crusty snow, a little gray rabbit came hopping as fast as he could into the grove of evergreens. The rabbit's furry sides heaved in panic. From beyond the hill came the howling of wild dogs in the thrill of the hunt. The bunny, his eyes wide with fright, frantically searched for cover. But the dark, cold trees lifted their branches artfully from the snow and frowned. They did not like this interruption of their quiet evening when growing was at its best.

Faster and faster the rabbit circled as the excited howling of the dogs sounded louder and louder.

And then Small Pine's heart shuddered. When the terrified rabbit ran near, Small Pine dipped its lower branches down, down, down to the snow. And in that instant before the wild dogs broke into the grove, the rabbit slipped under Small Pine's evergreen screen. He huddled safely among the comforting branches while the dogs galloped by and disappeared into the forest.

In the morning the rabbit went home to his burrow, and Small Pine tried to lift its lower branches back up to their proper height. It strained and struggled, but the branches had been pressed down too long through the night. *Oh well*, Small Pine thought, *no matter*. Perhaps the woodsmen wouldn't notice a few uneven branches near the ground in a tree so beautiful.

Several days later a terrible blizzard lashed the land. No one remembered ever having so much wind and snow. Villagers slammed their shutters tight while birds and animals huddled in their nests and dens.

A brown mother wren had become lost in the storm. With feathers so wet she could barely fly, she went from one large evergreen to another looking for a shelter. But each tree she approached feared the wren would ruin its perfect shape and clenched its branches tight, like a fist.

Finally, the exhausted wren fluttered toward Small Pine. Once more Small Pine's heart opened and so did its branches. The mother wren nestled on a branch near the top, secure at last. But when the storm ended and the bird had flown away, Small Pine could not move its top branches back into their perfect shape.

In them would be a gap evermore.

Days passed and winter deepened. The packed snow had frozen so hard that the deer in the forest could not reach the tender ground moss, which they ate to survive. Only the older, stronger deer could dig through the icy snow with their hooves.

One little fawn had wandered away from his mother. Now he was starving. He inched into the pine grove and noticed the soft, tender evergreen tips. He tried to nibble on them, but every tree quickly withdrew its needles so the tiny deer teeth couldn't chew them.

Thin and weak, he staggered against Small Pine. Pity filled the tree's heart and it stretched out its soft needles for the starving fawn to eat. But alas, when the deer was strong enough to scamper away, Small Pine's branches looked very ragged.

Small Pine wilted in sorrow. It could hear what the larger, still-perfect trees were saying about how bad it looked. A tear of pine gum oozed from the tip of a branch. Small Pine knew it could never hope for the honor of being the Queen's Christmas tree.

Lost in despair, Small Pine did not see the good Queen come with the woodsmen into the forest. It was the first Saturday of Advent, and she had come to choose the finest tree herself because this was a special celebration year in the history of her kingdom.

As the royal sleigh, drawn by two white horses, slowly passed through the forest, her careful eye scanned the evergreens. Each one was hoping to be the royal choice.

When the Queen saw Small Pine, a flush of anger filled her. How could such an ugly tree with so many drooping branches and gaps be allowed in the royal forest? She decided to have a woodsman cut it to throw away and nodded for the sleigh to drive on.

But then . . . she raised her hand for the sleigh to stop and glanced back at the forlorn little pine.

She noticed the tracks of small animals under its uneven needles. She saw a wren's feather caught in its branches. And, as she studied the gaping hole in its side and its ragged shape, understanding filled her heart.

"This is the one," she said, and pointed to Small Pine. The woodsmen gasped, but they did as the Queen directed.

To the astonishment of all the evergreens in the forest, Small Pine was carried away to the great hall in the castle. There it was decorated with shimmering, silver stars and golden angels, which sparkled and flashed in the light of thousands of glowing candles.

On Christmas Day a huge Yule log blazed in the fireplace at the end of the great hall. While orange flames chuckled and crackled, the Queen's family and all the villagers danced and sang together around Small Pine. And everyone who danced and sang around it said that Small Pine was the finest Christmas tree yet. For in looking at its drooping, nibbled branches, they saw the protecting arm of their father or the comforting lap of a mother. And some, like the wise Queen, saw the love of Christ expressed on earth.

So if you walk among evergreens today, you will find, along with rabbits, birds, and other happy living things, many trees like Small Pine. You will see a drooping limb, which gives cover, a gap offering a warm resting place, or branches ragged from feeding hungry animals.

For, as have many of us, the trees have learned that living for the sake of others makes us most beautiful in the eyes of God.